NINJA, GO!

Contents

World of Ninjago

Welcome to Ninjago!
Five brave Ninja protect
this magical land.
Their names are Cole, Jay,
Kai, Zane, and Lloyd.

They are masters of a
martial art called Spinjitzu.
The Ninja possess powers
of the four Elements of Ninjago.
These are Earth, Lightning,
Fire, and Ice.

Ninja, No More

The Ninja are sad.
Zane went missing after
a battle with an enemy.

Where could Zane be?
The Ninja do not feel
like a team without him,
so they split up.

Kai

This red Ninja is
the Master of Fire.
He has a hot temper!
Now that the Ninja team
has split up, Kai works
as a show fighter.
He thrills the audience
with his acrobatic moves.

Jay

Skillful Jay is the
Master of Lightning.
This blue Ninja is super
fast and adventurous.
Now that the Ninja team
has split up, Jay works
as a game show host.
His jokes make the
audience laugh!

Cole

This black Ninja is
the Master of Earth.
He is very strong and calm.
Now that the Ninja team
has split up, Cole works
as a lumberjack.
Chopping down trees
keeps him busy.

Lloyd Garmadon

This green Ninja is the
Master of all Elements.
He is upset that the
team split up.
He does not want to
get another job.
Lloyd still wants to be
a Ninja more than anything!

Zane

Zane is the Ninja of Ice.
He is a quiet and serious robot.
The other Ninja think that
Zane has been destroyed,
but he has rebuilt himself.
Where has he gone?
Will he ever see
his friends again?

NINJA WEAPONS

JAY

GOLDEN STRIKER

Description: Three-pointed dagger

Use: Sharp jabs in close combat

ZANE

SHURIKENS OF ICE

Description: Throwing stars

Use: Spin towards target with extreme force

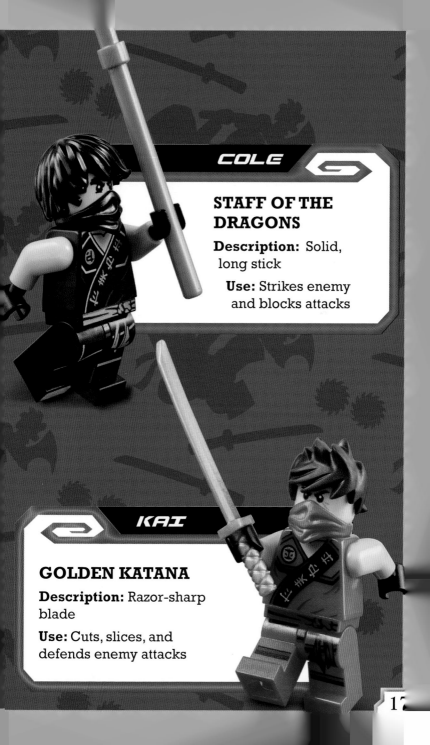

COLE

STAFF OF THE DRAGONS

Description: Solid, long stick

Use: Strikes enemy and blocks attacks

KAI

GOLDEN KATANA

Description: Razor-sharp blade

Use: Cuts, slices, and defends enemy attacks

Master Wu

Master Wu is a wise
and good teacher.
He taught the Ninja
all of their skills.

Garmadon

Garmadon is Master
Wu's brother. He used
to be evil, but now
he is good.

NINJAGO TIMES

Volume 12

GARMADON WRITES BOOK

Garmadon has written a book about his exciting life. We asked him to tell us more!

Can you tell us more about your transformation from bad to good?

I was a wicked dark lord. I told lies and even plotted to take over Ninjago! Now instead of fighting the Ninja, I spend my time training them.

REMEMBERING ZANE: New statue for much missed Ninja built in town center.

MYSTERIOUS POSTERS: Master Chen's followers put up posters in Ninjago. A special report.

Why did you change?

My son, Lloyd, and my brother, Wu, changed me with their goodness. I owe them my life.

Do you have a message for our readers?

I hope my story inspires other villains to give up their life of crime and live in harmony. Peace out!

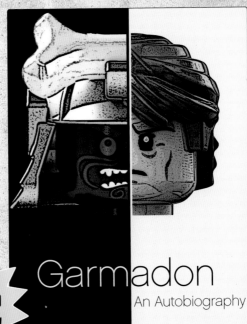

Garmadon
An Autobiography

MY JOURNEY FROM EVIL TO GOOD

Master Chen

This villain is Master Chen.
He wants to turn people into
snakes called Anacondrai!
To do this, he must steal
the powers of the Ninja.
So he invites them to a
contest on his island.

Master Chen
presents:

THE TOURNAMENT OF ELEMENTS!

Are you the most powerful warrior in Ninjago?

Come to Master Chen's island to prove it!

BE THERE

(Bring this flyer for one free bowl of noodles)

Nya

Nya is Kai's younger sister.
She is very clever.
Nya thinks that the
tournament is a trap!
She follows the Ninja
to Master Chen's island.
She hopes she will find
Zane there, too.

TOURNAMENT ARENA

Welcome to Master Chen's tournament arena. The Ninja find that it is full of surprise obstacles. Enter at your own risk!

Swerve to sidestep the falling swords.

Dodge spinning blades!

Don't fall down the trapdoor leading to the fire prison!

28

SPINJITZU

Spinjitzu is an ancient form of martial art. A Master of Spinjitzu can spin so fast that he turns into a powerful tornado of energy.

Dash past poison dart missiles.

Watch out for this dangerous deck of daggers!

Skylor

Skylor is Chen's daughter.
She can steal the power
of any Ninja she touches.
Chen wants her to steal
the powers of the Ninja.
But when she meets Kai,
she wants to be friends
with them instead!

Clouse

Evil Clouse has a Book of Magic.
He uses a magic spell to help
Chen turn people into snakes.
It even works on Garmadon!

Pythor

Pythor has always been a snake.
Master Chen needs his help
to make Clouse's magic spell
last forever.

CHEN'S EVIL PLAN

Master Chen's follower, Eyezor, is devoted but dim. He is still confused about Chen's plan to defeat the Ninja and conquer Ninjago.

What is this book?

It contains a spell t turn anyone I choos into Anacondrai. Ha ha ha!

Who are these Anacon... Anaconds?

Anacondrai, you foo They're the most feared of all the Serpentine tribes.

Anacondrai Army

Master Chen is now the leader
of a huge Anacondrai army!
He thinks nothing can stop
his plan to take over Ninjago.
But Garmadon still has a
good heart, even as a snake!
He uses a spell from the Book
of Magic to send Chen and
the Anacondrai far away.

Ninja Reunion

The Anacondrai are beaten!
Master Chen is gone for good.
But what really makes the Ninja
happy is seeing Zane again!

He was a prisoner on Chen's
island, but now he is free.
All five Ninja are back together.
Where will their adventures
take them next?

Quiz

1. Where do the Ninja live?

2. Which martial art have the Ninja mastered?

3. What does Kai work as after the Ninja split up?

4. Who is this Ninja in green?

5. What is Zane's element?

6. Where is Master Chen holding the Tournament of Elements?

7. Who is Lloyd's
   father?

8. Who is Nya's brother?

9. What power does Skylor have?

10. Who is this white and
    purple snake?

Answers on page 43

Glossary

Martial art   A form of fighting or self-defense

Acrobatic   Quick and flexible

Skillful   Having the ability to do something well

Autobiography   Book written by a person on the subject of his or her life

Tournament   A series of contests between a number of competitors

Obstacle   An object that blocks one's way

Reunion   Meeting up with a person or people after being separated for a period of time

Index

Answers to the quiz on pages 40 and 41:
1. Ninjago 2. Spinjitzu 3. Show fighter 4. Lloyd Garmadon
5. Ice 6. On his island 7. Garmadon 8. Kai
9. She can steal the Ninja's powers 10. Pythor

Penguin
Random
House

Editors Emma Grange, Himani Khatreja, Eleanor Rose
Designer Jenny Edwards
Assistant Art Editor Akansha Jain
Senior Art Editor Jo Connor
DTP Designers Umesh Singh Rawat, Rajdeep Singh
Pre-Production Producer Siu Yin Chan
Producer Louise Daly
Managing Editors Paula Regan, Chitra Subramanyam
Design Managers Guy Harvey, Neha Ahuja
Creative Manager Sarah Harland
Art Director Lisa Lanzarini
Publisher Julie Ferris
Publishing Director Simon Beecroft

Reading Consultant Linda B. Gambrell, Ph.D

Dorling Kindersley would like to thank
Randi Sørensen, Paul Hansford, and Robert Stefan Ekblom
at the LEGO Group.

This edition published in 2016
First American Edition, 2015
Published in the United States by DK Publishing
345 Hudson Street, New York, New York 10014
DK, a Division of Penguin Random House LLC

Page design copyright © 2016 Dorling Kindersley Limited

001–299988–Aug/16

A catalog record for this book
is available from the Library of Congress.

ISBN: 978-5-0010-1437-9

Printed and bound in China

www.LEGO.com
www.dk.com

A WORLD OF IDEAS:
SEE ALL THERE IS TO KNOW